The Sheffield and Tinsley Canal

Sheffield East End History Trail 1

Text

Simon Ogden

The **Hallamshire** Press 1997

THE TERMINAL WAREHOUSE IN THE 1820S

THE SHEFFIELD AND TINSLEY CANAL

Sheffield East End History Trail 1

© 1997 The Hallamshire Press

Published by The Hallamshire Press
The Hallamshire Press is an imprint of
Interleaf Productions Limited
Broom Hall
8–10 Broomhall Road
Sheffield S10 2DR
UK

Typeset by Interleaf Productions Limited
Printed in Spain by Edelvives

British Library Cataloguing in Publication Data
A catalogue record for this book is available from the British Library

ISBN 1 87418 26 1

Contents

The Story of the Canal   10

Construction of the Canal   15

Boats & Cargo   17

SECTION ONE
The Basin to Cadman Street   19

SECTION TWO
Cadman Street to Bacon Lane   28

SECTION THREE
Bacon Lane to the Aqueduct   35

SECTION FOUR
The Aqueduct to Broughton Lane   40

SECTION FIVE
Broughton Lane to Tinsley Locks   44

SECTION SIX
Tinsley Top Locks to River Don   49

Places of Interest along the Route   52

Further Reading   54

Introduction

....

Sheffield's East End has seen huge changes in the last 25 years. Thousands of houses, whole streets of people and vast works have disappeared, and enormous landmark buildings, new landscapes and different kinds of jobs have sprung up in their place. However, the evidence of the East End's rich and fascinating history is still all around if you know where to look.

At the same time the area is a greener and more pleasant place to walk around than it has been for well over a century, thanks partly to the opening up or improvement of a network of footpaths criss-crossing the valley, including the Canal Towpath and the Five Weirs Walk.

This series of East End Trails is intended to encourage you to explore the area on foot and to enjoy discovering the best of both the old and the new.

Main picture—Sheffield Basin and Park Goods Yard in the 1950s—Sheaf Works (now Sheaf Quay Pub) can be seen beyond the Goods Yard

This map shows the complete route of this East End Trail along the Sheffield and Tinsley Canal and back along the River Don including the *Five Weirs Walk* (see East End Trail 3). There are access points at regular intervals along the towpath, so the trail can be picked up and left, or walked in its entirety. This guide takes you section by section along the Sheffield and Tinsley Canal. Section maps indicate disabled access, toilets, bus and Supertram stops, and refreshment facilities as well as points of interest. For a cycling permit for the towpath, apply to: British Waterways Board, Lock Lane, Castleford, West Yorkshire, WF10 2LH. The annual fee is £1.00.

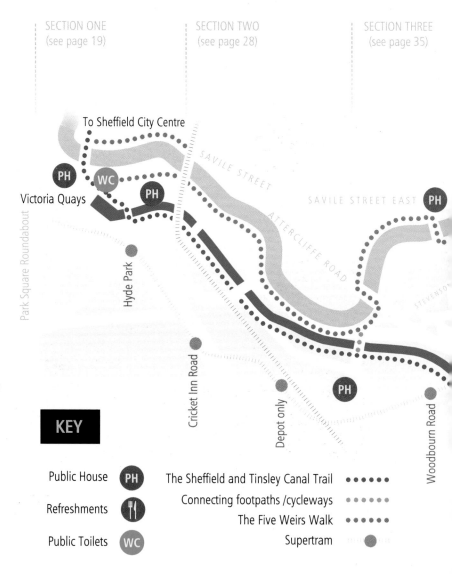

SECTION ONE
(see page 19)

SECTION TWO
(see page 28)

SECTION THREE
(see page 35)

To Sheffield City Centre

Victoria Quays

Park Square Roundabout

Hyde Park

Cricket Inn Road

Depot only

Woodbourn Road

SAVILE STREET

SAVILE STREET EAST

ATTERCLIFFE ROAD

STEVENSON

KEY

Public House	PH	
Refreshments		
Public Toilets	WC	

The Sheffield and Tinsley Canal Trail • • • • •
Connecting footpaths /cycleways • • • • •
The Five Weirs Walk • • • • •
Supertram ●

The **SHEFFIELD** *and* **TINSLEY CANAL**

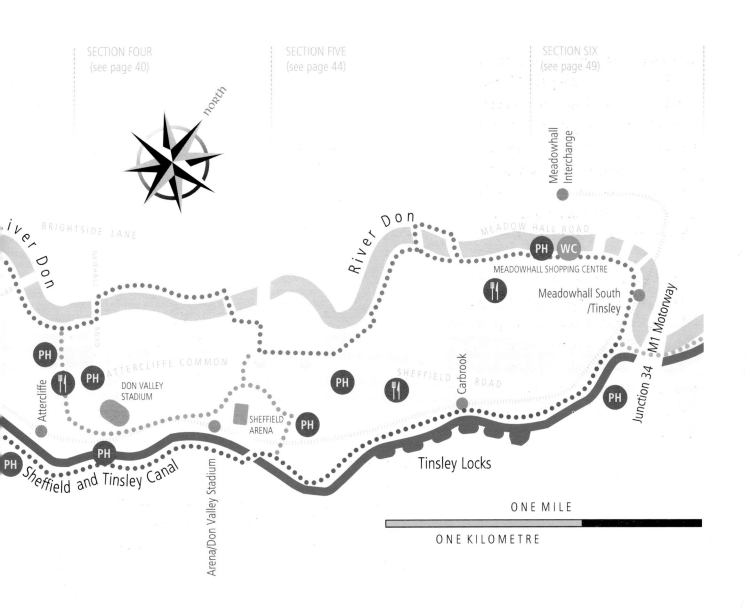

SECTION FOUR
(see page 40)

SECTION FIVE
(see page 44)

SECTION SIX
(see page 49)

north

BRIGHTSIDE LANE

River Don

River Don

MEADOW HALL ROAD

Meadowhall
Interchange

PH WC

MEADOWHALL SHOPPING CENTRE

Meadowhall South
/Tinsley

PH

ATTERCLIFFE COMMON

PH

Attercliffe

PH

DON VALLEY
STADIUM

SHEFFIELD
ARENA

PH

PH

SHEFFIELD

Carbrook

ROAD

PH

Junction 34

M1 Motorway

PH

PH

Sheffield and Tinsley Canal

Arena/Don Valley Stadium

Tinsley Locks

ONE MILE

ONE KILOMETRE

The **SHEFFIELD** *and* **TINSLEY CANAL**

On 22nd February, 1819, a huge crowd of 60,000 Sheffielders turned out to watch, as one excited journalist reported; 'a spectacle never before witnessed by human beings - a floating conveyance arriving in Sheffield'. In fact eleven 'floating conveyances' including the steam ship 'Industry' arrived, in convoy, at the Canal Basin to mark the opening of the Sheffield and Tinsley.

The boats were loaded with prominent citizens, a cannon which was fired frequently, and of course, a brass band. After the opening there was a procession round the town with the Masons, Oddfellows and 'Sick Clubs' (Trade Unions as such were illegal at this time) displaying their banners, followed by general celebration in all the pubs and hotels.

Thus was achieved a cherished ambition to connect land-locked Sheffield to the sea, via the Trent and Humber, which had first been proposed 120 years before in 1697. This proposal and further attempts by Doncaster Corporation (1704) and the Sheffield Cutlers Company (1721) were all defeated by the opposition of mill operators on the River Don, who feared interference with their source of water power and above all by the powerful Dukes of Norfolk, who owned most of the mills and also monopolised the local coal trade.

One of the main benefits of the canal was access to the cheap coal of South Yorkshire and this meant competition with the Dukes' own Sheffield Coal Company. For a hundred years successive Dukes, therefore, used their influence in Parliament to oppose a canal. They did however, concede that the River Don could be made navigable up to the borders of their manor at Tinsley. Work began in 1726

THE STORY OF THE CANAL

The **SHEFFIELD** and **TINSLEY CANAL**

BELOW - VICTORIA QUAYS

on the 'Dun Navigation', deepening the river and bypassing obstructions with short canals.

By 1751 boats could reach Tinsley. For the next seventy years Tinsley Wharf became the port of Sheffield, and all goods were unloaded there and brought to Sheffield by road, a highly unsatisfactory arrangement.

Finally came the Napoleonic Wars and with them a boom for South Yorkshire's cutlers and iron masters, producing swords, bayonets and cannon balls for the army. The

RIGHT - KEEL ENTERING 'BOAT HOLE' OF TERMINAL WAREHOUSE - 1960'S pressure for improved transport became too great and the Duke finally agreed to support a Canal Bill enacted in 1815. He did, however, insist that it followed a route which would connect with his collieries at Darnall and the Park, which involved locks and cuttings

Five years later, the canal was open for traffic, but in a much-changed economic climate. The war had ended at the battle of Waterloo in 1815 and trade had slumped. Much of the digging of the canal was carried out by the many unemployed of the town. The opening ceremony in 1819 was one of the few bright spots in a grim year.

Trade revived again in the 1820's and the canal prospered but this prosperity was short-lived. Having been delayed for so long, it enjoyed only twenty years of operation before the new railways began to take away its traffic. The opening of the Sheffield to Rotherham railway in 1838 halved its income in five years.

In 1845 the first big railway company, soon to be known as the Manchester, Sheffield and Lincolnshire, arrived in the town. Within two years it had gained control of the Sheffield Canal Company, partly for its large warehouse at the Canal Wharf but mainly to control the potential competition. Many other canal companies suffered the same fate at this time.

For the next fifty years the canal was operated increasingly as the poor relation to the railway, starved of maintenance and investment and only carrying traffic considered unprofitable by the M.S.L.R.

The situation improved when in 1889 a consortium of local industrialists and the Corporation forced a Bill through Parliament to separate the canal from direct railway control. A new company, The Sheffield and South Yorkshire Navigation Co., was set up in 1895 to run the whole waterway

The SHEFFIELD and TINSLEY CANAL

from Sheffield to the Humber. Plans were proposed for a new 'Sheffield Ship Canal' terminating in Attercliffe. New warehouses were built at Sheffield and the canal was promoted vigorously. Ultimate ownership, however, remained in the hands of the railway.

The First World War dealt another blow. The canal was nationalised and many of its boats were commandeered by the army to be used as troop transports on the canals of Flanders. No improvements were made during the war, and afterwards the canal was returned to an impoverished Canal Company. Sadly, many of the boats were not returned.

Sheffield's First Town Plan of 1924 envisaged modernisation of the canal with a new basin at Tinsley adjacent to the big steelworks, but the company could not raise the funds and traffic declined further. Nationalisation in 1948 came too late for the Sheffield and Tinsley.

The **SHEFFIELD** *and* **TINSLEY CANAL**

Some trade continued right up to the early 1970s. After that the Sheffield Canal, classified as a 'remainder waterway', languished in neglect, although further downstream below Rotherham, the South Yorkshire Navigation was being modernised and widened and is still a commercial waterway.

Now, however, there is renewed interest in the canal, not so much as a commercial waterway but for its recreational and amenity value. The improved canal and towpath forms the spine of a new 'Linear Park' which stretches from the City Centre to Tinsley and links Victoria Quays, East End Park and Meadowhall, and will eventually reach Rotherham. New uses and activities are being found for the Canal Basin.

Nowadays, we usually stand in awe of Victorian enterprise and business acumen, but it has to be said that the Sheffield-Tinsley canal was not an outstanding business success, vital though it was to the development of the town's industry. Vested interest delayed it for too long, and once built it was too quickly taken over by commercial rivals who deliberately arrested its development.

Despite this, it has continued to inspire excitement and interest in Sheffielders both as an economic asset and as a place with a special atmosphere.

VICTORIA QUAYS FESTIVAL 1995

The **SHEFFIELD** and **TINSLEY CANAL**

Construction of the Canal

The biggest problem which faced William Chapman, the Geordie engineer who designed the canal, was to arrange a water supply which did not deprive the numerous water-driven factories in Sheffield of their power; a fear which had caused opposition to previous canal proposals.

The problem had defeated earlier engineers but Chapman solved it ingeniously. He used water pumped from the workings of two nearby coalmines and from two streams too small to work water wheels; the Carbrook and the Acres Hill Dyke.

Politics dictated that a route south of the River Don be taken, since this allowed for a short branch-canal called 'the Greenland Arm' to connect to the Duke of Norfolk's coal mines at Darnall and to terminate at the Norfolk Coal Yard thereby winning the Duke's support.

A 'NAVVY' READY FOR THE TRAMP TO THE NEXT JOB. IN ADDITION TO ALL HIS TOOLS, INCLUDING BARROW, HE ALSO CARRIES A CUTLASS!

Chapman's estimate for the five mile waterway, including twelve locks, fifteen bridges and an aqueduct was £48,000. The final cost of £102,541, shows that overspending is not a purely modern vice!

The Canal at Tinsley Pump House - 1960s and 1990s

The **SHEFFIELD** *and* **TINSLEY CANAL**

Boats & Cargo

When completed, the new canal ran through open fields and skirted the small village at Attercliffe in a deep cutting, whence came much of the stone for the locks and edgings. The entire construction was carried out with pick and shovel, horse and wheelbarrow.

Some of the labourers would have been hard-living professional 'navvies' who tramped from job to job carrying their wooden wheelbarrows on their backs. Many more however were local cutlery and iron workers, forced to work on the excavation in return for a meagre unemployment pay. Ironically the 1987 canal refurbishment was carried out by 50 unemployed people on an Government scheme, as were improvements in the 1920s.

Not surprisingly, one of the main cargoes arriving in Sheffield was iron of a special high quality mined in Sweden. Another was coal, from the growing South Yorkshire coalfield. Together iron and coal fuelled the crucible holes and steel furnaces of the town.

Lime, timber, sugar and grain all came in bulk to the canal basin or to private wharves along the canal bank. Down to the sea went finished steel, cutlery, tools and machinery. Not all of it went to Hull. Going via Barnsley and Leeds a boat could reach Liverpool and some cargoes for America went this way.

In Yorkshire and the North East, canal boats were known as 'keels' not barges

ABOVE - A TYPICAL SHEFFIELD KEEL - 'THE DOROTHY PAX' - NOW BEING RESTORED AT SHEFFIELD BASIN

The **SHEFFIELD** and **TINSLEY CANAL**

and a Yorkshire keel was a distinctive boat. At 61'6" × 15'3" it was much broader than a Midlands 'narrow boat'. It was round-ended fore and aft with a mast and two square sails, making it look from a distance rather like a Viking longboat, from which it was descended.

When the sail could not be used, a horse generally pulled the keel. Extra horses could be hired from individuals known quaintly as 'horse-marines'. Only in the 1920s were engines introduced.

The Canal Companies themselves did not operate keels. This was left to the 'Bye-traders', some of whom ran quite large fleets, whilst others were operated by owner-captains. The boat families, men, women and children all worked hard—in lean times they would dispense with the hire of a horse and bow-haul the keel themselves.

Although keel folk always kept a house, often in one of the canalside communities like Staniforth or Thorne,

INSIDE THE CABIN OF KEEL 'BEATRICE' 1905. BEHIND THE CHILD IS A TINY CUPBOARD-LIKE BED, CURTAINED OFF IN THE DAY TIME. COOKING WAS DONE ON THE HOB OF THE OPEN FIRE.

at least a part of the family would live on board in the tiny cabins with their numerous lockers and small coal fires.

The children attended a variety of schools along the way and so gained a sketchy formal education, but made up for this by the worldly wisdom gained from their constant travelling.

The SHEFFIELD and TINSLEY CANAL

THE BASIN TO CADMAN STREET

Begin the trail on Exchange Place (2) facing the magnificent five storey Terminal Warehouse, (1) built in 1819 as the final destination of the canal. When it was constructed it faced onto a public square called the New Hay Market, with the Corn Exchange almost opposite and surrounded by the City's open markets.

Now the space is dominated by traffic, but when the Inner Ring Road is completed the City planners hope to restore the area to pedestrians and local traffic.

The main facade of the terminal was partly obscured until recently by the 1895 South Yorkshire Navigation Company offices, demolished in 1993. Through the central arch you can see the 'boat hole' which allowed 'dry'

cargoes such as sugar, fruit or tinned food to be hoisted from keels directly up to the various floors. The hoist equipment is still preserved in the top floor. Note also the spiral chute for loading wagons with sacks.

Round the corner to the right of the Terminal is Wharf Street. Here can be seen the original offices for the Basin, a small two-storey brick extension, curiously tacked on to the main warehouse and partly blocking doors and windows. There is no obvious explanation for this quirky siting.

After early initiatives by the City Council in the 1980s, the whole group of historic warehouses, together with the basin itself, were restored and brought back into use in 1993-95 by a partnership led by the Sheffield Development Corporation and British Waterways.

Still on Wharf Street, at right angles to the Terminal, is a short three-storey

The **SHEFFIELD** *and* **TINSLEY CANAL**

Ponds Forge International
Sports Centre

Sheaf Market

Trail Starts here

Castlegate

Blonk Street

Exchange Street

Park Square
Roundabout

PH

2

11 1

10 3

4

WC

9

5

BUSES
available here

north

R I V E R   D O N

Frank Cobb's
Howard Works

CANAL BASIN

Victoria Station Road

Furnival Road

Royal Victoria
Hotel

**RAMP
ACCESS**
to the canal here

FB

P

Swing Bridge

12

7

Basinmaster's
Office

Blast Lane

8

PH

13

6

Wicker Viaduct

A57 Sheffield Parkway

KEY TO THE MAPS

The Sheffield and Tinsley Canal Trail ● ● ● ● ● ● ●
The Five Weirs Walk ● ● ● ● ● ● ● ● ●
Cycle Track ● ● ● ● ●
Railway |||||||||||||||||
Supertram
Walkway

Place of interest referred to in text 12

Public House PH

Refreshments

Footbridge FB

Public Toilet WC

Victoria Railway Viaduct

'Dorothy Pax'

Cadman Street

Sussex Street

16

15 14

ACCESS
to the canal here

TO SECTION 2

The **SHEFFIELD** *and* **TINSLEY CANAL**

terrace (11), built around 1853 as the head office of the Tinsley Park Coal Company, an important customer of the canal. It was partly owned by the Huntsman family, descendents of Benjamin Huntsman, the inventor of crucible steel. Leaving Wharf Street, walk back round the Terminal towards a curving two-storey stone terrace(4). This looks like a row of tiny cottages, but was actually built as offices for coal and lime merchants, as part of the Park Goods Yard complex constructed by the Manchester, Sheffield and Lincoln Railway in 1851.

Beyond the terrace, take the steps (or ramp, reached from the Exchange Street side), up to the top of the stone arches (5). You are now on a small fragment of the Park Goods Yard which once comprised dozens of railway sidings covering the area as far as Furnival Road at first floor level. The site is now occupied by the Stakis Hotel and new offices. *(see illustration behind Introduction)*

Below, the remaining arches are all that is left of a labyrinth of stone vaulted warehouses into which goods and materials were lowered from the wagons above.

This vast structure was itself only part of the extensive complex of high-level railway lines and arches thrown across the Don Valley by the Manchester, Sheffield and Lincolnshire Railway between 1848 and 1853, which also included the Wicker Viaduct, the Victoria Station and Hotel and the Station Approach, all carried on 48 stone arches. This was the largest masonry viaduct in Europe at the time.

The example of the M.S.L. Railway was followed by the London and N.W. Railway which built its own City Goods Yard and a huge warehouse to the South of the Canal, where the Parkway now runs.

From then until the 1960s this was the hub of Sheffield's goods transport network, The Nunnery, Wicker and Bridgehouses Goods Yards were all nearby.

The **SHEFFIELD** *and* **TINSLEY CANAL**

Descending to the canalside again, you can now look into the inner basin, contained by three 'listed' warehouses, the Terminal (1), the Grain (3) and the Straddle (9). The two latter were added after 1895 as part of the renaissance enjoyed by the canal through the establishment of the South Yorkshire Navigation Company. On the south quay, open-sided sheds for timber and steel were formerly located.

The Straddle warehouse literally straddles the canal and goods could be hauled from boats through trap doors in each floor. The Grain warehouse was later converted, in 1925, to house 35 huge hoppers for grains and animal feeds, the bottoms of which have been retained and make up the ceiling of the pub on the ground floor. Notice the 'bucket hoist' used to convey loose grains from the boats to the hoppers.

Follow the edge of the canal round towards the swing bridge leading to the south side. The original granite and sandstone setts of the quayside have been mixed with new stone pavings to create smooth areas allowing for wheelchair access, and to mark vehicle areas.

Note the modern wetdock and next to it a ramp and chute used to load loose materials into the keels. Beyond this is the Dry Dock (12), constructed in the decade after 1819 presumably to facilitate the repair and perhaps building of keels.

In the later 19th Century it was filled in, probably to create more storage space and was only rediscovered in 1989 and excavated in 1994.

The swing bridge leading to the south side of the canal replaces an earlier one on the same site. The Basin Manager's House and Office was built by British Waterways in 1994/5 as part of the basin's restoration. Looking back into the basin, notice how the level of the quayside has been raised by adding a second course of coping stones, probably to increase the amount of water which could be stored in the upper level of the canal, or to counteract mining subsidence.

The **SHEFFIELD** *and* **TINSLEY CANAL**

Following the towpath we soon come to newly created mooring areas. At certain times these will be locked for security purposes. The towpath route will then be via Blast Lane, reached by ramp or steps next to the Basin Manager's House.

Blast Lane was so-named because it originally led from the town centre to the Park Blast Furnaces which were said to have lit up the whole area at night. The canal itself severed this road and the northern section of Blast Lane was renamed Effingham Road.

On the right of Blast Lane was the site of Sheffield Colliery (13), which

Vega Bermejo's Sculpture 'Sacred Cow' with Basin Master's Office behind

The **SHEFFIELD** *and* **TINSLEY CANAL**

THE BASIN AND TERMINAL WAREHOUSE IN THE 1820S. THE UNLIKELY 'MASTS' ARE ACTUALLY DERRICKS USED TO LIFT CARGOES INTO THE BOATS.

featured in many Victorian views of the City. The Inner Ring Road now occupies part of this site. Before leaving the canalside, study the view across to the North Quay.

The stone arches of the Park Goods Yard, now containing a modern car park, once converged on a railway bridge crossing the canal. The blue-brick support of this bridge can still be seen on the south side towpath.

Beyond is Sheaf Works House (8), which appears rather like a Derbyshire country house, dropped into industrial Sheffield. Actually it was the head office and warehouse of Sheaf Works,

The SHEFFIELD *and* TINSLEY CANAL

SHEAF WORKS, NOW SHEAF QUAY PUB

the first large steelworks in Sheffield to dispense entirely with water power and rely on steam alone. Built between 1822 and 1826 it was also the first factory to make use of the newly opened Sheffield and Tinsley Canal.

The works once stretched along both sides of the canal as far as Cadman Bridge (see illustration on front cover) and another part of it still survives now known as Sipelia Works (16). William Greaves and Co. who built the works brought in Swedish bar iron and coal and exported finished tools and cutlery via the new canal. Many of their products went to the 19th century settlers of North and South America.

The **SHEFFIELD** and **TINSLEY CANAL**

It is interesting to observe that the original principal entrance to Sheaf Works House (including the Time House and Weighbridge) faces the canal, not the road. One of Sheaf Works chimneys survives between the ring road and the railway.

If you are on Blast Lane go through a narrow stone arch in the side of the railway bridge and on to the towpath. Immediately you are under the Railway Viaduct (6). As you will see there is in fact an older, more handsome stone arch sandwiched between later stone and iron extensions.

It was the building of this railway viaduct in 1849 (running East to Grimsby and West to Manchester via the Woodhead Tunnel) which presaged the end of prosperity for the Sheffield Canal. The opening of the Sheffield to Rotherham Railway, in 1838, had already halved the canal's income in five years.

On the far side of the bridge the canal flows beside a curving factory wall (16) with a very substantial stone plinth and mooring rings with, further on, an archway leading to underground coal stores. All of these buildings were once part of William Greaves' Sheaf Works.

During working hours the earth-shaking sound of a nearby drop forge can be heard. Many people in Sheffield's East End grew up with forges like these almost in their back yards, often working day and night. Some swore they could not sleep without them! Now they are quite a rare sound.

On the opposite bank is the Sheffield Canal Company, the only working boatyard on the Sheffield-Tinsley Canal and home of the Princess Mary trip boat which operates as a water bus in the summer.

The Dorothy Pax, last remaining timber-built keel on the canal, is being restored here before being moved to the Basin to become a floating museum.

The **SHEFFIELD** and **TINSLEY CANAL**

Next comes Cadman Street Bridge (14), also known as 'Oblique Bridge' from its angle. It is one of the original fifteen canal bridges built in 1819.

Note the deep grooves in the masonry which have been worn by the horses' tow ropes over the years.

If you examine the wall on the opposite bank you will see that it is partly built out of whole grindstones. It is topped with split grindstones. Victorian industries never threw anything away if they could help it!

CANAL WORKS, CADMAN STREET

On the other side of the bridge is a ramp leading to Cadman Street.

A detour can be made up the ramp to admire two typical Victorian steelworks which face each other across the street. Canal Works (15), dating from around 1855, is a modest establishment, much altered but retaining its small cramped yard and archway. Across the street the Sipelia Works (16) are, by contrast, full of mid-Victorian pride and confidence. They even seem to have been built for a taller race of people.

SECTION TWO

CADMAN STREET TO BACON LANE

Passing over Cadman Bridge and turning right onto Sussex Street under the railway bridge, you will come to the old 'North Pole' pub (17). Set back from the street on the right it was probably built as the master's house for the Park Blast Furnaces. Now converted to offices, this once elegant early 19th century house predates the canal. Once known as Parkside Cottage it had a garden running down to a broad mill dam adjoining the River Don, which powered the bellows of the iron works.

Back on the towpath, the first feature on the far bank is the ruin of a once-handsome building (19). This was Parker's Wharf, built in the 1840s by Samuel Parker to take in cargoes of horn and ivory which were used extensively for handles in the cutlery trade.

The next bridge is the 1870 Midland Railway (20), still carrying trains from Midland Station to Barnsley, Leeds and York. It too has been widened. On the towpath are mooring rings.

Once through the bridge the view was, until recently, dominated by a tall gaunt black grain elevator (21), once

THIS SKETCH PROBABLY REPRESENTS THE OLD BERNARD ROAD BRIDGE. IN THE FOREGROUND IS THE CORPORATION YARD WHILST BEYOND THE BRIDGE CAN BE SEEN CEMENTATION FURNACES AND CHIMNEYS OF THE NAVIGATION WORKS, NOW PART OF BEDFORD STEELS YARD.

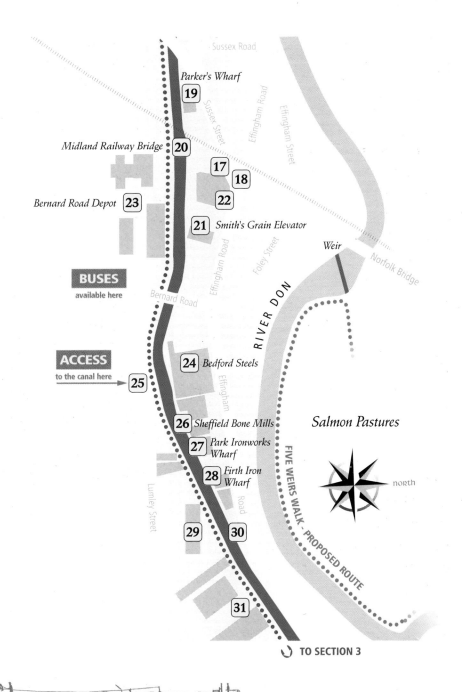

Parker's Wharf
19

Midland Railway Bridge · **20**

17
18

Bernard Road Depot **23**

22

21 Smith's Grain Elevator

Sussex Road

Sussex Street

Effingham Road

Effingham Street

Effingham Road

Foley Street

Weir

Norfolk Bridge

BUSES
available here

Bernard Road

Effingham

ACCESS
to the canal here

25

24 Bedford Steels

26 Sheffield Bone Mills

27 Park Ironworks Wharf

28 Firth Iron Wharf

Lumley Street

Effingham Road

RIVER DON

Salmon Pastures

FIVE WEIRS WALK - PROPOSED ROUTE

north

29   **30**

31

↻ TO SECTION 3

The **SHEFFIELD** *and* **TINSLEY CANAL**

operated by Samuel Smith, Provision Merchant. Grain was drawn out of boats and then later released into waiting carts and lorries. Opinions differ as to whether this structure was an ugly leftover or a fine industrial landmark but now it has been substantially demolished by its owners.

Just beyond the elevator site you can glimpse a factory with elegant round-topped windows (22). This was once a common feature of industrial buildings in the valley but is now rare, like the round-fronted pubs, found at acute angles between roads. On the towpath side a high wall bounds Bernard Road Depot (23), one of the first Corporation yards, set up in the 1890s. Materials for road construction would be delivered either from the canal or from the railway on the other side of the yard. Now the site is dominated by the refuse incinerator with its massive chimney where heat and electricity are generated from the City's rubbish.

Pass under Bernard Road Bridge (named after Bernard Edward, Duke of Norfolk). On the opposite bank is Bedford's Steelworks (24) which once had its own wharf. During working

A HAND-PASSED ROLLING MILL. MOST SHEFFIELD ROLLING MILLS ARE AUTOMATED THESE DAYS, BUT A FEW SPECIALISED MILLS ARE STILL OPERATED BY TONGS AND MUSCLE POWER.

hours you can peer into the open-sided rolling mill where mill-hands still manipulate long strips of red-hot steel with tongs in the traditional manner.

Steps lead up to Lumley Street here (25).

Next to the rolling mill is an interesting four-storey building with arched windows. This attractive building had a prosaic purpose, it was a bone mill, probably making fertiliser (26).

Next to the bone mill is a small inlet (27). Once this was large enough to take a boat, and led to a tunnel under Effingham Road, presumably so that cargoes could be unloaded directly to the nearby Park Iron Works.

A short way on we come to two brick buildings on the off-side, with a series of arches now bricked up (28), this was Firth's Iron Wharf. In its heyday, before the First World War it would

FORMER BONE MILLS, NOW PART OF BEDFORD ROLLING MILLS

The **SHEFFIELD** and **TINSLEY CANAL**

FIRTH IRON WHARF WITH KEELS UNLOADING - LATE 19TH CENTURY

Don, to coke ovens and coal heaps on Salmon Pastures. That part of Sheffield was for 150 years an absurdly-named spot, blackened with slag heaps and polluted water. Now, as you can see, the River Don and its banks become cleaner each year and the prospects of salmon and pastures are once again a possibility.

have been stacked to the roof with Swedish Dannemora iron bars, unloaded from the keels through the archways, and later transported by horse and cart to Savile Street to feed the hungry furnaces of the Atlas Works.

On the towpath we now come to the stone abutments of a demolished bridge (29). This used to carry a tramway from the Nunnery Colliery, near the present Parkway Avenue, across the canal, Effingham Road and the River

Here it is easy to appreciate that the canal is built on an embankment some

AN INTERCITY TRAIN THUNDERS BY ON THE MIDLAND RAILWAY BRIDGE

The SHEFFIELD and TINSLEY CANAL

ten feet above the valley floor. On the opposite bank are sluice gates built to drain the canal very rapidly into the river in the event of the embankment being breached, as it was in the 1940 blitz (30). The River Don flows by but on a lower level through Salmon Pastures and can be accessed by the Five Weirs Walk.

Anyone brought up in Sheffield's East End will remember the vivid orange colour of canal water. The source of this was the outlet marked by a hump in the towpath (31). It allowed water to be pumped out of the underground workings of the Sheffield Nunnery Colliery, this water was stained orange by ochre in the workings but it helped maintain the level in the canal.

THE 'EYE OF THE NEEDLE' - BACON LANE BRIDGE WAS NOTORIOUSLY DIFFICULT TO NEGOTIATE

In 1987 British Coal abandoned the pumps and the alternative supply of water pumped from the river was increased, thus eliminating this source of pollution. As a result more fish, plants and insects have flourished in the cleaner water.

THE CANAL BEFORE RESTORATION IN 1975

Passing several more canalside works (note mooring rings on the wall) Bacon Lane Bridge is reached (32). This is another original 1819 Bridge. Canal people called it 'The Needle's Eye'. It was so low that at times of high water, boats had to be crow-barred through it as damage to the soffit shows. On the far side are steps leading to Bacon Lane.

The **SHEFFIELD** *and* **TINSLEY CANAL**

Another detour is possible here, to see the Baltic Works and its unique memorial. Turn right at the top of the steps and then right again on to Effingham Road. The newly restored building painted red is the Baltic Works built by the steel firm of Beardshaws around 1850 (33). The illustration shows how it looked 130 years ago with keels on the canal. Parts of the original facade have been removed since then, but the arched entrance, quaint old timehouse and board room above with stained glass windows all survive, as do many of the original workshops round the (private) works yard. All have been refurbished to create small workshops.

Beyond the works gate on Effingham Road look for a plaque set into the factory wall. It is a unique monument to the twenty-nine men, women and children killed in the first and only Zeppelin bombing raid on Sheffield on the night of 26th September, 1916. Thirty-six bombs were dropped, many of them falling on close-packed houses nearby. Sheffield, for long the 'arsenal of Europe' had its first bitter taste of modern warfare that night.

Following the green markers you can also join the Five Weirs Walk from Effingham Road. Returning to Bacon Bridge those requiring refreshment may carry straight up Bacon Lane to the Woodbourn Inn (34). Beyond is the Woodbourn Athletics Centre completed in 1987.

The **SHEFFIELD** *and* **TINSLEY CANAL**

THE BALTIC WORKS MEMORIAL

BALTIC WORKS FROM THE CANAL

BACON LANE TO THE AQUEDUCT

Returning to the towpath, look at the back of Baltic Works. The new owners have divided it into small workshops, but have preserved the crucible chimney—a wide stack at right angles to the canal containing several flues. Crucible steelmaking was invented in Sheffield in the 1740s by Benjamin Huntsman. This process formed the foundation of Sheffield's steel industry, and indeed of all steel industries throughout the world.

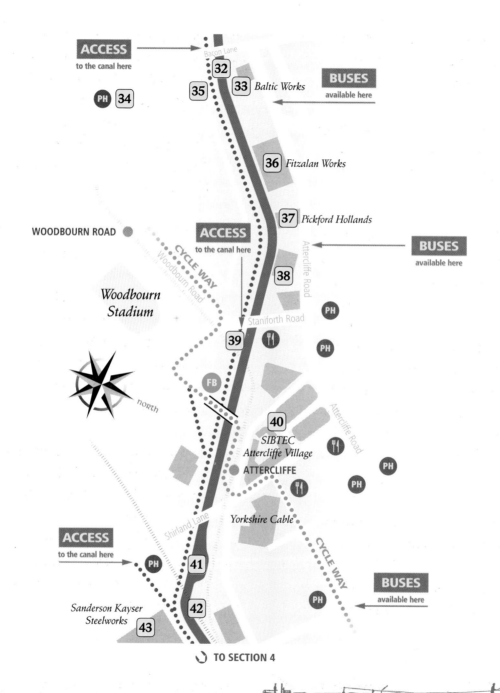

ACCESS
to the canal here

32

35   33 *Baltic Works*

BUSES
available here

PH 34

36 *Fitzalan Works*

37 *Pickford Hollands*

ACCESS
to the canal here

38

BUSES
available here

WOODBOURN ROAD

CYCLE WAY

Woodbourn
Stadium

Staniforth Road

39

PH

PH

north

FB

40
*SIBTEC
Attercliffe Village*

ATTERCLIFFE

PH

PH

PH

Yorkshire Cable

Shirland Lane

CYCLE WAY

ACCESS
to the canal here

PH

41

BUSES
available here

PH

*Sanderson Kayser
Steelworks*

42

43

TO SECTION 4

The **SHEFFIELD** *and* **TINSLEY CANAL**

Baltic Works was named after its main source of iron, the Swedish Baltic ports, to which it was linked via the canal.

On the towpath just past the bridge is a white-painted cast-iron post (35) indicating three miles to Tinsley.

Next to Baltic Works is Fitzalan Works (36), for many years associated with Cocker Brothers, but founded in 1839 by the steel maker George Marriott. Amongst his claims to fame, he was one of the first men in Sheffield to adopt the newfangled London fashion of full-length trousers, rather than knee-breeches and stockings. His workmen were apparently much amused and called them 'britches wi' chimbly pipes on em'. They probably also said they'd never catch on.

Beyond Fitzalan Works is Pickford Holland's brick yard, which once also had its own wharf (37). John Brown had a wharf here where iron from his mines in Asturias, Spain was unloaded.

Next comes Spartan Steels, a newly-cleaned works which spans both sides of the canal, linked by a footbridge (38). Founded by one Jabez Shipman, a steelmaster and local Councillor in the 1890s, the works has a fine Victorian facade facing Attercliffe Road, which has recently been refurbished.

Attercliffe Road can now be reached by climbing the steps or ramp just under Pinfold Bridge (39) and turning right on to Staniforth Road. Those seeking refreshment will find numerous pubs, cafes and restaurants on Attercliffe Road, which is particularly noted for Asian cuisine. A bargain or two can be picked up in Attercliffe shops.

Beyond Pinfold Bridge the canal changes character dramatically. We find ourselves in the deep 'Attercliffe Cut' on which hundreds of unemployed laboured between 1815 and 1819. In summer the sides are covered in green, but in winter the exposed rock strata present a graphic picture of local geology.

The **SHEFFIELD** and **TINSLEY CANAL**

ATTERCLIFFE CUT WITH NEW CYCLE BRIDGE

Although there are fewer buildings of interest, this is made up for by a far greater opportunity to observe birds, fish and plants and wider views over the valley.

The 'Pinfold' which gave its name to the bridge was a pen in which the stray animals of Attercliffe were impounded in the pre-industrial era, to be released only by payment of a fine to the 'Pinder' Most households then kept at least a pig and these were amongst the most frequent guests of the Pinfold!

Until the 1970s, the cut was lined with terraced houses. The canal became a favourite place to dump rubbish and many boats sustained damage by

The **SHEFFIELD** and **TINSLEY CANAL**

hitting submerged objects such as gas cookers and even safes!

Now this whole area has been laid out for advanced technology industry (40) and new housing, forming the core of the New Attercliffe Village.

Pinfold Bridge also virtually marks the extent of canalside factory building in Sheffield. Though you will see many more works, you will notice that most were built to take advantage of nearby railways or roads, rather than the canal.

The new bridges carry the Supertram and a cycle/footway over the canal. Both reflect traditional canal bridge design.

When the canal was built, the Attercliffe and Tinsley areas were dotted with small coal mines and there were numerous loading points for coal, often brought to the water by tramways.

Passing under Shirland Lane bridge

(note the remains of the 1819 bridge, under the 1953 one), we come to a wide pool called a 'winding hole' where boats could turn or several boats could moor astern (41). Iron bar may once have been unloaded for the famous nearby Huntsman Steelworks near here. The pool was also a favourite swimming pool for generations of Attercliffe kids. Now pass under the M.S.L.R. railway bridge of 1864.

On the far side of the canal the massive brick walls which tower above us mark the site of Attercliffe Station which closed in 1927. The entrance to the subway under the railway can still be seen (42).

To the right of the towpath, once again high on an embankment, you can look down into the former Sanderson Kayser's steel works, and peer into the melting shop, once lit by flames from the furnaces (43).

The canal now crosses Darnall Road on a sturdy stone aqueduct of 1819

The **SHEFFIELD** and **TINSLEY CANAL**

(known to many generations as 'T' Acky Dock') (44). It is listed as an Ancient Monument and can best be viewed by descending the path to Darnall Road.

The aqueduct was built to span the Attercliffe to Worksop Turnpike. The road beyond is still known as Worksop Road. By following Worksop Road for approximately 200 yards you will reach several pubs, restaurants and cafes.

BARTON AQUEDUCT - THE FIRST CANAL AQUEDUCT IN BRITAIN

THE AQUEDUCT TO BROUGHTON LANE

Remount to the towpath. The canal skirts what was once the site of Brown Bayley's steelworks, built in 1871 but now dismantled to create the East End Park, containing Don Valley Stadium and Bowl and the Sheffield Arena.

The Park has its own moorings and a new bridge giving access to the towpath. The next bridge we come to is Coleridge Road, formerly Pot House Lane after the old Attercliffe Common Pottery. The road was re-named not after the famous poet, but for Bernard Coleridge, Attercliffe's first MP. The present bridge was built as part of a work-creation programme during the 1930s depression.

The works on the right, before the bridge (46), once belonged to the Huntsman steel firm and still contains a crucible shop.

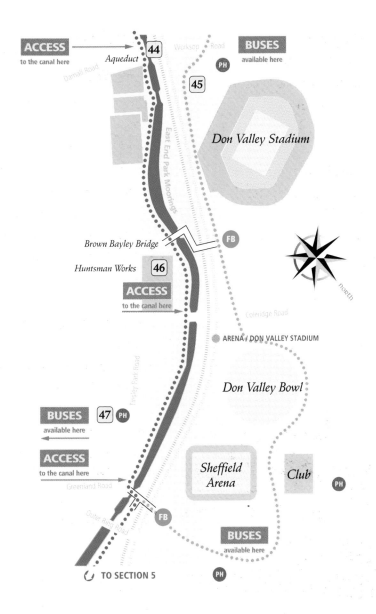

ACCESS
to the canal here

44

Aqueduct

Darnall Road

Worksop Road

BUSES
available here

PH

45

East End Park Moorings

Don Valley Stadium

Brown Bayley Bridge

FB

Huntsman Works **46**

ACCESS
to the canal here

Coleridge Road

ARENA / DON VALLEY STADIUM

Don Valley Bowl

Tinsley Park Road

BUSES
available here **47** PH

ACCESS
to the canal here

Greenland Road

Sheffield Arena

Club

PH

Outer Ring Road

FB

BUSES
available here

↺ **TO SECTION 5**

PH

north

The **SHEFFIELD** and **TINSLEY CANAL**

THE DON VALLEY STADIUM VIEWED FROM THE EAST END PARK MOORINGS

From the towpath can be seen a 'scrap basket' from Stocksbridge Steelworks, now converted to a viewing platform for the Don Valley Bowl.

After Coleridge Road comes a new footbridge taking the towpath over to the north bank. This bridge stands on the site of the old Broughton Lane Bridge.

The new Broughton Lane Bridge carries the Outer Ring Road over the canal and railway.

To the left is Broughton Lane, surely the only street in Sheffield named after a convicted criminal. He was the highwayman Spence Broughton who, with an accomplice, robbed a post boy on lonely Attercliffe Common nearby in 1795. The next year he was caught, tried and hanged at York. His body was returned to the scene of his crime and 'hung in chains' from a gibbet, where it reputedly remained for many years. Broughton was apparently the last man

FORMER ALLIANCE FORGE (LATER BALFOUR DRAWINGS) LETTERHEAD SHOWING 'GREENLAND ARM' CANAL TO RIGHT.

The SHEFFIELD and TINSLEY CANAL

in England to be punished in this gruesome fashion. As well as in Broughton Lane his name is remembered in the famous folk song 'Spencer the Rover'. His chains are now in Weston Park Museum.

To the right of the bridge is Greenland Road, marking the former junction of a short branch canal called the 'Greenland Arm' built to connect with the Duke of Norfolk's coal mines at Darnall. When it fell into disuse it was filled in to become part of the modern Greenland Road.

There are three pubs nearby, The Gibbet and the Stadium on Broughton Lane and the Friendship (47) on Tinsley Park Road. The Gibbet has a small collection of Spence Broughton memorabilia.

The next part of the canal runs through an area once dominated by coal mining and the land is marked by old spoil heaps. One platform of the old Broughton Lane Station remained until recently. During the 1893 Miners Strike, on 7th September, a pitched battle took place here between a thousand-strong picket 'composed principally of women and reckless youths' and a detachment of the Dublin Fusiliers sent from Hillsborough Barracks. On the same day a similar clash at Featherstone resulted in the shooting dead of two miners.

Soon we come to the remains of Peacock Bridge (48), a wooden railway bridge with an iron mechanism which allowed it to be raised to let boats through. This was originally built to carry coal wagons from the nearby Tinsley Park Collieries. It is hoped to

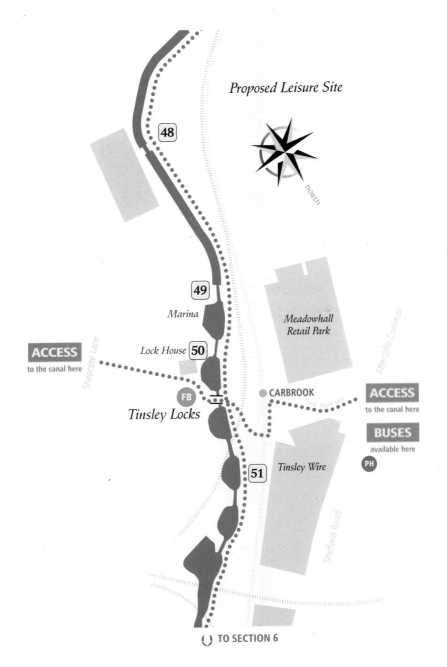

Proposed Leisure Site

north

[48]

[49]

Marina

Lock House [50]

Meadowhall
Retail Park

Attercliffe Common

ACCESS
to the canal here

Shepcote Lane

FB

CARBROOK

ACCESS
to the canal here

Tinsley Locks

[51]

BUSES
available here

PH

Tinsley Wire

Sheffield Road

⊔ **TO SECTION 6**

The **SHEFFIELD** *and* **TINSLEY CANAL**

restore this bridge in the future. Next to it was a wharf where coal was loaded into special coal barges.

Now we arrive at Tinsley Top Lock (49) which, despite its industrial setting and dredging tip, is one of the most attractive parts of the canal. The series of broad, placid pools, built as reservoirs for the locks, give it an atmosphere of stillness amid the bustle.

This area is being developed as a permanent mooring site by British Waterways. On the right of the canal stand two modern lock keepers' houses (50). A modern bridge leads to Shepcote Lane. On the left a path leads under the railway to Lockhouse Lane

THE REMAINS OF PEACOCK BRIDGE

The **SHEFFIELD** *and* **TINSLEY CANAL**

CANAL BOATS AND LOCK HOUSE

picturesque old lock house which stood by it. A short length of rail marks where a steam crane used to stand.

Next to this lock is another iron marker (51) indicating one mile to Tinsley. The extensive Tinsley Wire Works spans both sides of the canal here.

and Attercliffe Common, where a supermarket, hot food outlets and the Commercial Inn can be found.

A plaque on No. 4 Lock reads 'Blitzed December 15th 1940', a small reminder of one of the devastating air raids suffered by the city in World War Two. The bombs also destroyed the

A FISHERMAN NETS A GRAYLING AT TINSLEY LOCKS

TINSLEY LOCKHOUSE CIRCA.1920

The waterway now begins a rapid descent to Tinsley via seven locks. There were once eight, but two in the series were combined into a single deep

lock to allow construction of a new railway bridge in 1963. Stones from the old lock can be seen piled on the tow path.

The construction of this new railway bridge also necessitated altering the course of the canal several yards to the north. Part of the old lock can be seen on the opposite bank. The new length of canal is contained by concrete slabs and steel sheet piling.

Tinsley Top Locks

The canal now curves towards Sheffield Road Bridge, where there is another lock. By crossing the canal at the lock you can gain access to a cafe and the Plumpers pub (52). There were two pubs of this name in the Lower Don Valley but no very satisfactory explanation of its origin! On the left the stone wall marks the old Great Central Railway Goods Depot.

Below the lock is Tinsley Turnpike Bridge. The original bridge carried the Turnpike Road of 1759 connecting Sheffield with the wharves at Tinsley. This Turnpike eventually became Attercliffe Road/Common/Sheffield Road.

Passing under the Bridge you come to the Pump Houses (53) for transferring water to the canal from the river, which again comes in to view. It is possible to access the Five Weirs Walk at this point, and the Meadowhall Centre and Supertram. Follow the signs.

TINSLEY ROLLING MILLS IN THE EARLY 20TH CENTURY

The scene is dominated by the double-decked Tinsley Viaduct, a monument to the daring but flawed civil engineering of the 1960s.

The **SHEFFIELD** *and* **TINSLEY CANAL**

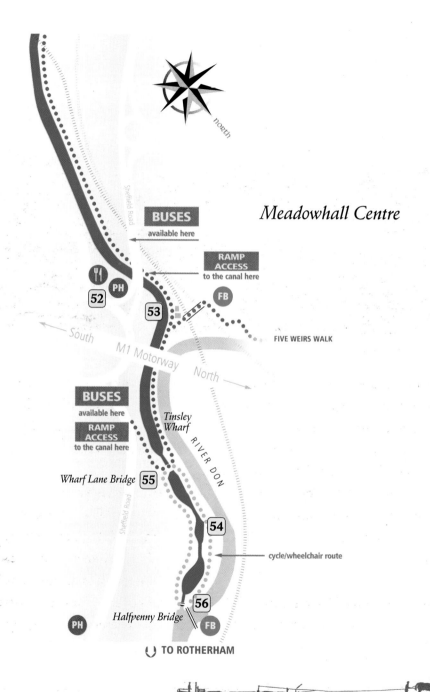

BUSES
available here

RAMP
ACCESS
to the canal here

Meadowhall Centre

PH

52

53

FB

FIVE WEIRS WALK

South

M1 Motorway

North

BUSES
available here

RAMP
ACCESS
to the canal here

*Tinsley
Wharf*

RIVER DON

Wharf Lane Bridge 55

54

cycle/wheelchair route

56

PH

Halfpenny Bridge

FB

TO ROTHERHAM

The **SHEFFIELD** *and* **TINSLEY CANAL**

THE OLD HALFPENNY BRIDGE

Beyond the Viaduct the towpath runs along a narrow spit of land between canal and river. Here was Tinsley Wharf (54), the once busy port of Sheffield for 70 years before the opening of the Sheffield-Tinsley Canal. Until recently Tinsley Rolling Mills operated here, on an island between River and Canal.

The small Wharf Lane Bridge (55) has been rebuilt but the rounded brick abutments of the original can clearly be seen underneath it. Cross over the Bridge to reach Tinsley shops and the Sheffield Road bus route.

Continuing along the towpath we pass the final flight of locks which bring us to the River Don. The Sheffield and Tinsley Canal terminates here, but the river itself is navigable as far as Jordan Weir, half a mile downstream, where the Sheffield and Keadby Canal

The SHEFFIELD and TINSLEY CANAL

continues by crossing the river on a long footbridge. This is known as Halfpenny Bridge (56). Until the late 1940s it was still a toll bridge, the name coming from the price of a ticket. Tolls were collected by an old man from a small hut. Many who passed by here every day to work became so accustomed to paying that they would push halfpennies under his door, even when he was off duty!

Our trail ends here, but the towpath to Rotherham offers another interesting walk by river and canal, much of it in surprisingly rural surroundings (see Trail 3, the Five Weirs Walk).

PLACES OF INTEREST ALONG THE ROUTE

1. Terminal Warehouse
2. Site of Corn Exchange
3. Canal Company Offices
4. Wharf Street Buildings
5. Coal Merchants Offices
6. Park Goods Arches
7. Wicker Viaduct
8. Royal Victoria Hotel
9. Sheaf Works
10. Straddle Warehouse
11. Grain Warehouse
12. Basin Manager's House
13. Site of Sheffield Colliery
14. Cadman Street Bridge
15. Canal Works
16. Sipelia Works
17. North Pole
18. Park Iron Works
19. Parker's Wharf
20. Midland Railway Bridge
21. Smith's Grain Elevator
22. Round Topped Windows
23. Bernard Road Depot
24. Bedford Steels
25. Lumley Street Steps
26. Sheffield Bone Mills

The **SHEFFIELD** *and* **TINSLEY CANAL**

27. Park Ironworks Wharf

28. Firth Iron Wharf

29. Nunnery Bridge

30. Sluice Gates

31. Nunnery Outlet

32. Bacon Lane Bridge

33. Baltic Works

34. Woodbourn Inn

35. Mile Post

36. Fitzalan Works

37. Pickford Hollands

38. Spartan Steel

39. Attercliffe Cut

40. Attercliffe Village & Technology Centre

41. Chippingham Street Basin

42. Atterclifffe Station

43. Sanderson Kayser

44. Aqueduct

45. East End Park Don Valley Stadium

46. Huntsman Works

47. Sheffield Arena

48. Peacock Bridge

49. Tinsley Top Locks Moorings

50. Lock Houses

51. Mile Post

52. Cafe and Plumpers Pub

53. Pump House

54. Tinsley Wharf

55. Wharf Lane Bridge

56. Halfpenny Bridge

For more information about Sheffield history, the Canal or the Lower Don Valley contact the following:

Local Studies Library, Central Library, Surrey Street, Sheffield S1 1XZ.
Tel: 0114 2734753

Sheffield Record Office, Shoreham Street, Sheffield S1.
Tel: 0114 2734756

Kelham Island Industrial Museum, Kelham Island, Sheffield S3 8RY.
Tel: 0114 2722106

Abbeydale Industrial Hamlet Museum, Abbeydale Road South, Sheffield S7 2QW.
Tel: 0114 2367731

Bishops' House, Meersbrook Park,

The **SHEFFIELD** *and* **TINSLEY CANAL**

Norton Lees Lane, Sheffield S8 9BE.
Tel: 0114 2557701

City Museum, Weston Park, Sheffield
S10 2TP.
Tel: 0114 768588

Tourist Information Centre, Town Hall,
Sheffield S1 2HH.
Tel: 0114 2734672

Department of Planning and Economic
Development, Town Hall, Surrey
Street, Sheffield S1 2HH

Inland Waterways Association (South
Yorkshire and Dukeries Branch)
132 Hadfield Street, Sheffield S6 3RS.
Tel: 0114 2334912

South Yorkshire Industrial History
Society,
Dora Cottage, Bakewell Road, Matlock
DE4 4EB.
(The history of Sheffield's industry and
trades)

FURTHER READING

GENERAL

The Waterways of Britain, a Social Panorama.
D. D. Gladwin. Batsford, 1976.
A Pictorial History of Canals.
D. D. Gladwin. Batsford, 1977.
A Pictorial History of Canal Craft.
P. L. Smith. Batsford, 1979.

LOCAL

Memories of the Sheffield & S. Yorkshire.
Mike Taylor. Yorkshire Waterway Publication, 1988.
The Canals of Yorkshire and N.E. England (2 vols.).
Charles Hadfield. David & Charles, 1972, 1973.
Sheffield Canal, an Archive Teaching Unit.
C. M. Butterworth, Sheffield City Council, 1970.
The Early History of the Don Navigation.
T. S. Willan. Manchester U.P. 1965.
A Life on the Humber.
Harry Fletcher. Faber, 1975.

Sheffield's Waterway to the Sea.
A. W. Goodfellow
(In transactions of Hunter
Archeological Society Vol 5. 1943
p246-253)
The Story of Old Attercliffe.
G. R. Vine 1932-36.
**Sheffield's East Enders: Life as it
was in the Lower Don Valley**
Keith Farnsworth, Sheffield City
Libraries, Nov. 1987.
**The Complete Guide to the
Sheffield and South Yorkshire
Navigation.**
The Hallamshire Press, 1995.
Humber Keels and Keelmen.
Fred Schofield
(Terence Dalton 1988)
Flying Sail.
Michael Ulyatt
(Mister Pye Books 1995)

Text by Simon Ogden
Design and photography by
Jonathan Ogilvie at Sheffield City
Council's Directorate of Planning and
Economic Development.
Other photography: Sheffield
Forgemasters, Ken Philip, Tony
Woodcock (Design and Building
Services.)
Footer illustration by Edward Paget-
Tomlinson.

There are two other *Sheffield East
End History Trails* published by
The Hallamshire Press:-
No. 2 *Attercliffe Village*
No. 3 *The Five Weirs Walk*

The SHEFFIELD *and* TINSLEY CANAL